The Family

The Castle

The Rooms

BLAIR CASTLE

FAMILY PEDIGREE OF

THE DUKES
OF ATHOLL

John Murray, 1st Duke of Atholl
b. 1660 d. 1724
m. Katherine Hamilton
m. Mary Ross

William
b. 1689 d. 1746

James 2nd Duke
b. 1690 d. 1764
m. Jean Lannoy
m. Jean Drummond

Jean

Charlotte

John 4th Duke
b. 1755 d. 1830
m. 1 Jane Cathcart
2 Marjory Forbes

James

George

George
b. 1761 d. 1803
m. Anne Grant

Charlotte   **Mary**

John 5th Duke
b. 1778 d. 1846

Amelia

James
b. 1782 d. 1837
m. Emily Percy

Edward   **Robert**   **Elizabeth**   **Frederick**   **Catherine**   **Charles**

John

George 6th Duke
b. 1814 d. 1864
m. Anne Home Drummond

Charlotte   **James**   **Frances**

George Edward
b. 1818 d. 1854
m. Penelope Pemberton

Anna   **Harriet**   **Caroline**

John 7th Duke
b. 1840 d. 1917
m. Louisa Moncrieffe

George Herbert
b. 1849 d. 1936
m. Helen Mulholland

Alice

Arthur Mordaunt

Dorothea   **Helen**   **Evelyn**

John 8th Duke
b. 1871 d. 1942
m. Katharine Ramsay

George

James, 9th Duke
b. 1879 d. 1957

George Evelyn
b. 1880 d. 1947
m. Muriel Beresford Hope

Irene

George Anthony
b. 1907 d. 1945
m. Angela Pearson

George Iain, 10th Duke
b. 1931 d. 1996

Photographs of the 2nd, 3rd, 5th, 6th and 7th Dukes courtesy of Ronald Weir

John, 1st Duke

James, 2nd Duke

John, 3rd Duke

John, 4th Duke

John, 5th Duke

George, 6th Duke

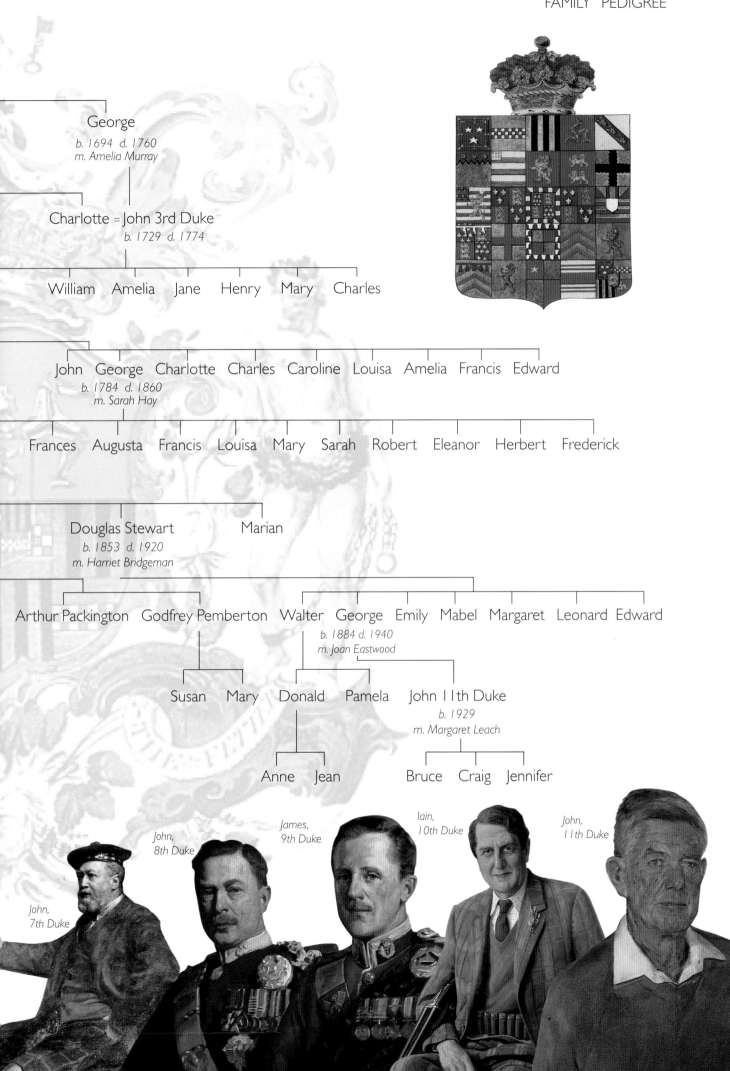

George
b. 1694 d. 1760
m. Amelia Murray

Charlotte = John 3rd Duke
b. 1729 d. 1774

William   Amelia   Jane   Henry   Mary   Charles

John   George   Charlotte   Charles   Caroline   Louisa   Amelia   Francis   Edward
b. 1784 d. 1860
m. Sarah Hay

Frances   Augusta   Francis   Louisa   Mary   Sarah   Robert   Eleanor   Herbert   Frederick

Douglas Stewart   Marian
b. 1853 d. 1920
m. Harriet Bridgeman

Arthur Packington   Godfrey Pemberton   Walter   George   Emily   Mabel   Margaret   Leonard   Edward
b. 1884 d. 1940
m. Joan Eastwood

Susan   Mary   Donald   Pamela   John 11th Duke
b. 1929
m. Margaret Leach

Anne   Jean   Bruce   Craig   Jennifer

John,
7th Duke

John,
8th Duke

James,
9th Duke

Iain,
10th Duke

John,
11th Duke

THE FAMILY

OVER NINETEEN GENERATIONS THE STEWARTS AND MURRAYS OF ATHOLL HAVE BACKED

SUPPOSED PORTRAIT OF JOHN, 1ST (MURRAY) EARL OF ATHOLL D. 1642

WINNERS AND LOSERS, BEEN IN AND OUT OF POLITICAL FAVOUR, WON BATTLES AND LOST THEM. THEY HAVE BEEN ADVENTURERS AND POLITICIANS, JACOBITES AND ROYALISTS, ENTREPRENEURS AND AGRICULTURALISTS, SOLDIERS AND SCHOLARS. AND THEY HAVE ALMOST ALL, IN ONE WAY OR ANOTHER, MADE THEIR MARK ON BLAIR CASTLE.

Early days

AN EARLY FAMILY COAT OF ARMS

The first of the present line was Sir John Stewart of Balvenie. Sir John was the half brother of King James II of Scotland, who rewarded him in 1457 with the Earldom of Atholl (the original Atholl family line had died out in the early 1300s).

The 1st Earl was a bold man who was sent to quell the troublesome Macdonalds of the Isles with the royal injunction *Furth fortune and fill the fetters*. A liberal translation might be *Get the chains on him and the future's yours* - which he did and it was. Not surprisingly, this became the family motto.

MARY QUEEN OF SCOTS

For several generations, Earl John's descendants lived as uneventfully as it was possible to in medieval Scotland. The 3rd Earl added a great hall to the castle, where his son, the 4th Earl, welcomed Mary Queen of Scots in 1564. Royal entertainment consisted of a hunt in nearby Glen Tilt at which they slew 360 deer and five wolves.

THE 1ST DUKE - A DETAIL FROM THE PORTRAIT ON THE PICTURE STAIRCASE

THE 1ST DUKE'S CHARTER

When the 5th Earl died without sons in 1595, there was a hiccup in the succession which was only resolved in 1629 when the title went to his grandson John. John's mother Dorothea had married Sir William Murray of Tullibardine. Thus, John became the 1st Murray Earl of Atholl and the title has remained in the Murray family ever since.

The dukedom

Following the Union of the Crowns in 1603, it was hard even for Highlanders to ignore events in England. During the Civil War, both the 1st Earl and his son the 2nd Earl were Royalists. Blair Castle became a prime target for Cromwell's forces. They captured it in 1652 and held it until Charles II was restored to the throne in 1660. For his loyalty to the crown, the 2nd Earl was made a marquis in 1676.

His son the 2nd Marquis continued to support the monarch, in the person of Queen Anne, and was duly rewarded with a dukedom in 1703. But the Queen also wanted the new Duke to put his weight behind the Act of Union between Scotland and England . This he refused to do until better terms were made available for Scotland. His obstinacy resulted in him being placed under house arrest at Blair Castle for several months in 1708.

Divided loyalties

With the Jacobite risings of 1715 and 1745, things became complicated for the family. The 1st Duke and his second son James supported the government; but the eldest and youngest sons, William and George, followed the Stewart cause. For his part in the 1715 uprising, William was stripped of his title and lands and exiled to France. His younger brother James duly became 2nd Duke on their father's death in 1724.

In 1745, William returned from France with Bonnie Prince Charlie and raised the Stewart standard at Glenfinnan. On the way south they stayed at Blair Castle, which had been sensibly vacated by James who remained loyal to the government and knew what his brothers were up to. Shortly afterwards, government forces again captured the castle.

LORD GEORGE MURRAY
B. 1694 - D. 1760
BY JEREMIAH DAVISON

Early in 1746 the third son, Lord George Murray, returned from commanding the Jacobite campaign in England, and turned his attention to the unusual task of besieging his own home. But before he could complete the job he was recalled to the disastrous battle of Culloden. He survived the battle but died in exile in Holland. His brother William died imprisoned in the Tower of London.

JAMES, THE 2ND
DUKE OF ATHOLL

THE THREE LEGS OF
THE ISLE OF MAN

The Manx connection

Their brother James, meanwhile, was lucky as well as canny. Through his grandmother, Lady Amelia Stanley, daughter of the 7th Earl of Derby, he had inherited the sovereignty of the Isle of Man. The resulting income from rents and patronage was put to good use when he returned to Blair Atholl after the '45 and continued with the alterations to the castle that had been interrupted by the uprising. By 1758 he had finished the work of remodelling it in the style of a grand Georgian mansion.

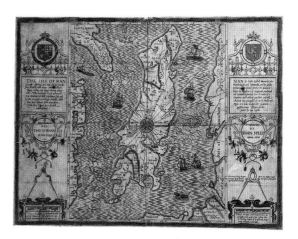

MAP OF THE ISLE OF MAN AS 'DESCRIBED BY
THOMAS DURHAM ANNO. 1595 AND PERFORMED BY JOHN SPEED ANNO. 1610'

5

LADY JEAN AND LADY CHARLOTTE

James had no sons, however, and since his eldest daughter had eloped to France with an elderly admirer and died there, the only way to keep the title in the family was to marry off his second daughter, Charlotte, to her first cousin. This cousin was John Murray, son of the exiled Lord George. John duly became 3rd Duke in 1764.

The 3rd Duke almost immediately sold the Manx sovereignty to the government, which was eager to bring the smuggler-infested island under its control.

'BRIG LARCH OF LONDON GOING OUT OF MALTA. ROBERT DOUGLASS COMMANDER 1824'

The sale raised £70,000 and enabled him to devote his energies to developing the grounds and woodlands at the family's second home, in Dunkeld.

His son, the 4th Duke, did even better from the Manx connection. In 1828 he sold the remaining properties and privileges for the astronomical sum of £417,000. This may have offset some of the losses incurred by an unlikely passion for larch, of which he had planted 25 million with a view to helping keep the British navy afloat. Alas, the first iron steamship set sail while they were still mere saplings.

For queen and country

The 5th Duke suffered ill health and his nephew, Lord Glenlyon, later the 6th Duke, was effectively in charge of things when Queen Victoria first visited Dunkeld, in 1842. Two years later Lord Glenlyon lent her Blair Castle for a three-week holiday. In appreciation of the vigilance of the guard of Athollmen who attended her, she granted the Duke and his men her colours, and so the right to bear arms. Thus the Atholl Highlanders became a private army. Today they are the only one remaining in Europe.

ORIGINAL ATHOLL HIGHLANDERS BANNER PRESENTED BY QUEEN VICTORIA IN 1845

Victoria's love of the Highlands helped encourage the spread of the railway. In 1863, the line passed through Atholl land on its way from Dunkeld to Inverness, bringing the 7th Duke a windfall of some £33,000. This went towards the transformation of Blair Castle from Georgian mansion to the Victorian baronial building we know today.

His son, known as Bardie from his title Marquis of Tullibardine, was a career soldier who saw action first in the Sudan and then in the Boer War in South Africa. There he raised the Scottish Horse, which he

BARDIE, THE 8TH DUKE

later commanded at Gallipoli in the First World War. He became 8th Duke in 1917 and his wife, Katharine Ramsay, who had brains and beauty in equal measure became first Scottish woman MP in 1923, and subsequently the first Conservative woman Minister of State.

George Herbert Murray, great uncle to the 11th Duke, great grandfather of the 10th Duke

The 8th and 9th Dukes, Bardie and his brother James, both died childless. So in 1957 the title moved sideways to Iain Murray, a direct descendant of the 3rd Duke. It was Iain, as 10th Duke and his mother, Angela, who turned Blair Castle into the major tourist attraction it is now. He was also President of the Scottish National Trust, Chairman of the Royal Lifeboat Institution and Chairman of The Westminster Press.

JAMES, THE 9TH DUKE

Modern times

The effects of war, death duties and economic depression brought the inevitable difficulties. In 1932 the estate was formed into a company and in 1936 the castle opened its doors to the public, one of the first private houses in Britain to do so. During the First World War it had been a hospital. Now, in the Second World War, it became home to a prep school and Glasgow evacuees.

THE HON. ANGELA CAMPBELL-PRESTON, MOTHER OF THE 10TH DUKE, BY BRYAN ORGAN

FOUR GENERATIONS OF THE FAMILY

KATHARINE RAMSAY 8TH DUCHESS

THE 10TH DUKE AND AN ATHOLL HIGHLANDER PROUDLY DISPLAYING QUEEN VICTORIA'S ORIGINAL BANNER

On the 10th Duke's death in 1996, also childless, the title again moved sideways, this time to his second cousin once removed, John Murray, who lives in South Africa. The 11th Duke, whose eldest son is the Marquis of Tullibardine, visits Blair Castle each year. The 10th Duke's half-sister, Sarah Troughton, lives with her family in the castle apartments and runs the castle and estate as a Trustee of the Blair Charitable Trust.

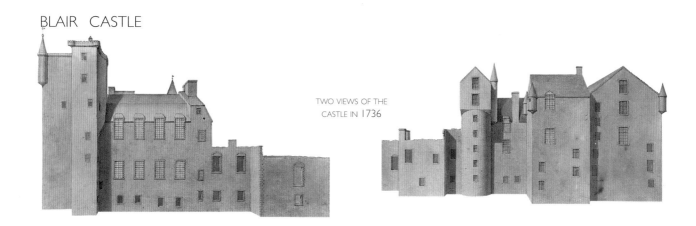

TWO VIEWS OF THE
CASTLE IN 1736

THE CASTLE

LIKE MOST VERY OLD HOUSES, BLAIR CASTLE HAS BEEN TRANSFORMED A NUMBER OF TIMES BY SUCCESSIVE GENERATIONS, AND IT IS NOW QUITE DIFFICULT, ESPECIALLY WHEN ONE IS INSIDE, TO TELL WHAT WAS BUILT WHEN.

But as the illustrations show, there have been three main ages of development: medieval, Georgian and Victorian. And with the new visitor facilities recently completed one might add a fourth, millennial.

In 1336, Edward III stayed in the tower on his way to raid the Highlands. But by 1564 and the arrival of the next royal visitor, Mary Queen of Scots, the castle had become larger and perhaps a little more comfortable. In 1530 the 3rd Earl had extended the building south from the tower with a great hall (now the dining room) built over a series of vaulted chambers.

THE EAST FRONT OF THE CASTLE IN 1864, BY WILLIAM EVANS, ART MASTER OF ETON
AND FRIEND AND TUTOR OF THE ATHOLL FAMILY

Cold and draughty

Records begin in the year 1269 when the Earl of the day returned from the Crusades to find that he had acquired a squatter. He wrote to the king complaining that a neighbour, John Cumming of Badenoch, had moved in while he was away and started building a tower on his land. But his protest was ineffectual, for seven hundred years later Cumming's Tower still stands, the oldest and tallest part of the castle.

CUMMING'S TOWER

Getting warmer

The next major change was begun in 1740 by the 2nd Duke and continued after the interruption of the '45, when his besieging brother Lord George Murray had put several cannon balls through the roof.

In keeping with the mood of the times, the architect James Winter removed the turrets and castellations and remodelled the castle as a Georgian mansion with pitched roofs, chimney stacks, and fine interiors by the stuccoist Thomas Clayton of Edinburgh.

BY THE TIME WILLIAM EVANS PAINTED THE HOUSE FOR A SECOND TIME, EIGHT YEARS LATER IN 1872, IT HAD BEEN TRANSFORMED FROM GEORGIAN MANSION TO VICTORIAN BARONIAL CASTLE

Central heating

Today, however, in its eighth century of existence, the castle is very much alive again. During the season it bustles with visitors, and throughout the year it also welcomes annual events such as the ceremony of the Keepers of the Quaich and the Glenfiddich World Piping Championship, along with private and corporate functions of all kinds.

A hundred years later dawned the great age of the Scottish baronial pile, for which Queen Victoria has much to answer. Happily the 7th Duke had a medieval original for inspiration and in the 1870s, with the help of Edinburgh architect David Bryce, he put back the tower and crenellations, built a new entrance hall and front gates, and crowned it all with a splendid ballroom. The 7th Duke also installed conveniences such as telephones, gas and bathrooms, and in 1908 built an estate hydro-electric scheme.

Aviemore Photographic

THE 11TH DUKE AND DUCHESS OF ATHOLL WITH HRH THE PRINCE OF WALES AT A *KEEPERS OF THE QUAICH* DINNER AT THE CASTLE

But for all the modernisation, the kitchen remained three floors below the dining room, at the opposite end of the house, and dinner tended to be lukewarm. In 1922, five years after the 7th Duke's death, the main part of the castle was let, and the family have since used the private apartments for their residence.

To reflect the demands of the times, the facilities have now been greatly improved. Architects Jamie Troughton and Hugh Broughton have developed a larger shop and a more spacious self-service restaurant. They have also constructed an exhibition hall, and an outside terrace. And to complete the 21st century visitor experience they have at last dispensed with the prehistoric plumbing that had plagued visitors and staff alike for so long. A fine thing is progress!

Entrance Hall

WHAT COULD BE MORE APPROPRIATE TO A CASTLE THAN AN ENTRANCE HALL THAT DOUBLES AS AN ORNAMENTAL ARMOURY? THIS WAS BUILT IN 1872 BY THE EDINBURGH ARCHITECT DAVID BRYCE AS PART OF THE 7TH DUKE'S SCHEME TO CONVERT THE GEORGIAN

THE STAG TILT WAS KEPT IN THE CASTLE GROUNDS UNTIL KILLED FIGHTING IN 1850, AGED 13. HIS ANTLERS FROM THE AGE OF THREE ONWARDS ARE MOUNTED IN THE PASSAGE BEYOND THE ENTRANCE HALL. THE FAMILY MOTTO, (TOP OF PAGE) 'FURTH FORTUNE AND FILL THE FETTERS', IS CARVED IN WOOD OVER THE FIREPLACE, WHICH IS SURROUNDED IN GLEN TILT MARBLE

MANSION BACK INTO A CASTLE AGAIN. WEAPONRY DISPLAYS WERE PART AND PARCEL OF THE VICTORIAN BARONIAL STYLE AND THIS ONE, WHICH INCLUDES TARGES AND MUSKETS USED AT THE BATTLE OF CULLODEN, WAS ASSEMBLED BY THE 7TH DUKE, A MODEL HIGHLAND LAIRD WHOSE INTEREST IN THINGS PAST LED HIM TO CHRONICLE THE FAMILY HISTORY.

LEFT: AN ATHOLL HIGHLANDER WITH THE STAG 'TILT' IN THE ENTRANCE HALL

The Stewart Room and Earl John's Room

WHEN THE 3RD EARL EXTENDED THE CASTLE IN 1530, HE BUILT A GREAT HALL WHICH WAS SUPPORTED BY THIS PAIR OF VAULTED CHAMBERS. THE FIRST OF THE TWO CHAMBERS WAS USED AT ONE STAGE AS A KITCHEN, AND WHEN THE 7TH DUKE CONVERTED IT TO HIS SMOKING ROOM IN THE 19TH CENTURY, HE FOUND OVENS TO THE LEFT OF THE FIREPLACE AND NEAR THE WINDOW ALCOVE. TODAY THE ROOMS COMMEMORATE THE LIFE AND TIMES OF THE ATHOLL FAMILY IN THE 16TH AND 17TH CENTURIES SUCCESSIVELY.

A MINIATURE OF MARY QUEEN OF SCOTS

THE CHAIRS ARE OF 17TH CENTURY SCOTTISH DESIGN. THE INITIALS AR STAND FOR ALEXANDER ROBERTSON OF LUDE, THE NEIGHBOURING ESTATE.

LADY DOROTHEA STEWART, THE 5TH EARL'S HEIRESS

THE CHITTARONE, A FORM OF LARGE LUTE, WAS MADE IN VERONA IN 1555. THE UNIQUE REGAL ORGAN IS DATED 1630.

THE STEWART ROOM

MARY QUEEN OF SCOTS AND HER SON JAMES VI – A PORTRAIT OF 1583

The Stewart Earls of Atholl were loyal supporters of Mary Queen of Scots. She visited the castle in 1564 and befriended the 4th Earl's wife, subsequently writing her a letter of condolence on her husband's death in 1579. The two double portraits show Mary with her son James VI and her parents James V and Mary of Guise. The miniatures in the case below are of Mary and Lady Dorothea Stewart, the 5th Earl's heiress.

Over the fireplace hangs a portrait of Dorothea's husband, Sir William Murray of Tullibardine, from whom the Murray Earls of Atholl are descended.

THE IVORY SPADE WAS BROUGHT BACK FROM CEYLON IN 1594 AS A PRESENT TO THE EARL OF TULLIBARDINE'S SISTER

EARL JOHN'S ROOM

Earl John was the 1st Murray Earl of Atholl. Both he and his son the 2nd Earl (later the 1st Marquis) were staunch royalists during the English Civil War. Their portraits hang on the window wall. Two other famous royalists also feature in this room.

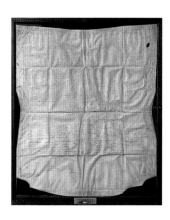

ONE OF FOUR ORIGINAL COPIES OF THE NATIONAL COVENANT OF 1638 IN WHICH THE SCOTTISH COVENANTERS PLEDGED TO RESIST POPERY, PRELACY AND SUPERSTITION.

THE BED WAS MADE IN 1650 FOR THE 1ST MARQUIS OF ATHOLL, AND THE CLOCK IS BY JOSEPH KNIBB, CLOCK-MAKER TO CHARLES II

Above the fire is the Marquis of Montrose who raised the king's standard at Blair in 1644 and five years later was hanged in Edinburgh. The helmet and breastplate (right), were worn by Viscount Dundee who was killed in his moment of victory over government forces at the battle of Killiecrankie, three miles south of Blair Atholl, in 1689.

HELMET AND BREASTPLATE BELONGING TO VISCOUNT DUNDEE WITH THE MEMORIAL ABOVE HIS VAULT, PLACED BY THE 7TH DUKE IN 1889

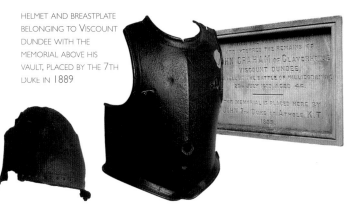

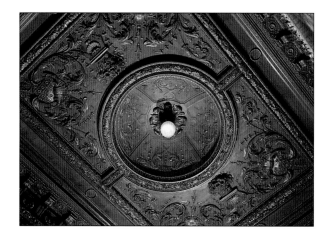

THE PLASTERWORK WAS ORIGINALLY WHITE AND GOLD IN COLOUR, BUT WAS PAINTED DURING THE VICTORIAN ALTERATIONS.

THE CHARTER FROM QUEEN ANNE, GRANTING THE 2ND MARQUIS HIS DUKEDOM.

THE 1ST MARQUIS OF ATHOLL BY JACOB DE WITT

photograph courtesy of Ronald Weir

The Picture Staircase

AS HIS PORTRAIT SUGGESTS, THE 2ND DUKE HAD A DISTINCT TASTE FOR GRANDEUR AND THIS STAIRCASE IS THE FIRST EVIDENCE OF IT. COMPLETED IN 1756, IT FORMS PART OF THE REMODELLING OF THE MEDIEVAL CASTLE AS A GEORGIAN MANSION BY THE ARCHITECT JAMES WINTER. THE PLASTERWORK WAS DONE BY THE EDINBURGH STUCCOIST THOMAS CLAYTON, ASSISTED BY ITALIAN CRAFTSMEN. THE 2ND DUKE WROTE A DETAILED MEMO ON THE ARRANGEMENT OF THE PICTURES FOR WHAT IS EFFECTIVELY A FAMILY PORTRAIT GALLERY.

Resplendent in the robes of the Order of the Thistle, the 2nd Duke gazes out from the top of the staircase. Even more resplendent as Julius Caesar, his grandfather, the 1st Marquis, was painted by Jacob de Witt. A small matter of some 1700 years did not deter de Witt from incorporating the battle of Bothwell Brig (1679) in full swing in the background.

Other notable portraits include his father, the 1st Duke, at Dunkeld House; his grandmother, Lady Amelia Stanley; her mother, Charlotte de la Tremouille; and a number of ancestors, some more prepossessing than others, including William of Orange.

LADY AMELIA STANLEY

CHARLES,
PRINCE OF
WALES,
AFTERWARDS
KING
CHARLES II

CHARLES,
LORD
STANLEY,
AFTERWARDS
8TH EARL OF
DERBY

The Small Drawing Room

MARBLE BUST OF
QUEEN CHARLOTTE,
WIFE OF GEORGE III

COSY IS NOT A WORD THAT THE 2ND DUKE'S ALTERATIONS IMMEDIATELY CALL TO MIND, BUT THIS WAS PROBABLY THE CLOSEST HE CAME TO HAVING A FAMILY ROOM. HERE ADULTS AND CHILDREN WOULD HAVE READ, PLAYED CARDS OR EMBROIDERED IN THE LIGHT REFLECTED FROM THE WINDOWS AND LAMPS BY THE HIGH MIRROR OVER THE FIREPLACE.

POLE SCREENS SHADED THE LADIES' FACES FROM THE FIRE TO AVOID THE
DISASTROUS EFFECT OF HEAT ON THEIR WAX-BASED MAKEUP

THE EIGHT MAHOGANY CHAIRS WITH FISHSCALE DECORATIONS COST
£26.10S IN 1756. THEY WERE SUPPLIED BY JOHN GORDON AND
EMBROIDERED BY JEAN DRUMMOND, THE 2ND DUKE'S SECOND WIFE

The room boasts more plasterwork by Thomas Clayton, a marble chimneypiece and supporting Ionic columns by Thomas Carter of London, and a carved overmantel by Charles Ross.

The lamp brackets on either side of the fire are fine examples of rococo design, as are the frames surrounding the portraits of Charles II (as Prince of Wales) and Charles Lord Stanley, both by Sir Peter Lely.

The Tea Room

TEA WAS STILL A RELATIVE LUXURY IN THE 2ND DUKE'S DAY, HENCE THE LOCKABLE TEAPOYS ON EITHER SIDE OF THE FIREPLACE. THE TAKING OF AFTERNOON TEA WOULD HAVE BEEN A REGULAR SOCIAL OCCASION DEMANDING AN APPROPRIATELY ELEGANT SETTING.

JAPANESE TEA SET

MAHOGANY TEAPOY

SÈVRES CHINA DISPLAY

Here there is more fine plasterwork, as well as an unusual frieze containing musical instruments in the section above the mantelpiece. The Chippendale and Sheraton cabinets contain a magnificent display of Sèvres china.

ELIZABETH, DAUGHTER OF JAMES VI, WHO MARRIED THE KING OF BOHEMIA AND WAS KNOWN AS THE WINTER QUEEN SINCE SHE RULED FOR ONLY SIX MONTHS

The damage was seamlessly repaired by Grandison of Peebles and the new, restored section is indistinguishable from what remains of the original stucco by Thomas Clayton. Clayton also made the elaborate overmantel, while the marble chimneypiece below was made by Thomas Carter in 1751.

The Dining Room

ALTHOUGH THIS SPLENDID ROOM IS STILL OCCASIONALLY USED FOR RECEPTIONS AND DINNER PARTIES, THERE WAS LUCKILY NO ONE DINING IN IT WHEN PART OF THE CEILING FELL DOWN IN 1985.

2ND DUKE'S WHISKY BOTTLE WITH A NINE PINT CAPACITY NOBLE GOBLET, OR TALLBOY

THE ATHOLL HIGHLANDER
COLOURS WERE ISSUED IN
1979 AND ARE USED ON
PARADE

The room was created in all its baroque grandeur from the 16th century great hall. The ceiling roundels of the four seasons are by Thomas Bardwell, and the local scenes in the wall panels by Charles Stewart, a local artist patronised by the 3rd Duke. One of the earliest Scottish landscape painters, Stewart was the brother of the maker of the musical clock in the Tearoom.

THE SILVER STAG MOUNTED ON GLEN TILT
MARBLE WAS A SILVER WEDDING GIFT TO THE
7TH DUKE AND DUCHESS FROM THE TENANTS
IN 1888. THE NINE-LEAF GEORGIAN
MAHOGANY DINING TABLE EXTENDS TO SEAT
24 PEOPLE. THE DINNER SERVICE IS
WORCESTER AND ROYAL WORCESTER.

CEILING ROUNDEL BY
THOMAS BARDWELL

19

MODEL LIFEBOAT PRESENTED TO THE 10TH DUKE

LEFT: IAIN, THE 10TH DUKE, PAINTED BY CARLOS SANCHA IN 1982 TO MARK THE TWENTY-FIFTH ANNIVERSARY OF HIS ASSUMPTION OF THE TITLE.

JOHN, THE 11TH DUKE OF ATHOLL BY BRENDON KELLY

The Anteroom

IN THE 2ND DUKE'S DAY AND LATER IT SEEMS LIKELY THAT ETIQUETTE WOULD HAVE REQUIRED THE FAMILY AND GUESTS TO PROCEED TO THE DINING ROOM IN ORDER OF PRECEDENCE. THE MAIN STAIRCASE WOULD HAVE LED THEM STRAIGHT TO THE ANTEROOM, WHERE THEY WOULD HAVE FOREGATHERED FOR THIS PURPOSE.

THE FUNERAL CORTEGE OF THE 8TH DUKE PASSING BY THE CASTLE IN 1942

Today the Anteroom houses an exhibition commemorating the life of Iain, the 10th Duke, who died in 1996. The case nearest the window shows aspects of his work including The Westminster Press of which he was chairman, Atholl Estates, and the Atholl Highlanders which he revived in 1966.

The second case contains items relating to his predecessors, the 8th and 9th Dukes, his own father who was killed in action in 1945, and his mother, Angela Campbell-Preston, who remarried and devoted herself to running the Atholl estates in the 1960s and 70s. The case concludes with the 11th Duke and his family.

The Blue Bedroom Suite

There are two particularly striking features to this attractive room. One is that it enjoys the rare luxury of a bathroom, one of three installed upstairs by the 7th Duke in 1885. The other is the marvellous full length portrait of his wife, Louisa Moncrieffe, one of a family of eight daughters, all of them celebrated Victorian beauties.

ABOVE CENTRE: NEEDLEWORK BY ANNE HOME DRUMMOND, 6TH DUCHESS, INCORPORATING HOLLY, THE BADGE OF HER OWN FAMILY, AND JUNIPER THE BADGE OF THE MURRAYS.

THE BATHROOM OF 1885

The Blue Bedroom is in the oldest part of the castle, although most of the furnishings – the Coromandel wood dressing table, work box and writing table for example - are from the 19th century. The adjoining dressing room is where, before the arrival of bathrooms, one would have bathed in front of the fire. The 6th Duchess was lady-in-waiting to Queen Victoria, hence the engravings of the royal family.

LOUISA MONCRIEFFE, 7TH DUCHESS

The Blue Dressing Room

RIGHT: 19TH CENTURY COURT MOURNING JEWELLERY IN
REAL AND IMITATION JET, WORN BY THE 6TH AND 7TH DUCHESSES

BELOW RIGHT: A FINE COLLECTION OF MAUCHLIN WARE.

BELOW: LOUIS PHILIPPE BONHEUR DU JOUR CABINET

The 4th Duke's Corridor

NAPOLEON DOMINATED EVENTS IN THE 4TH
DUKE'S DAY. THE MARBLE BUSTS ARE OF
WELLINGTON, BLUCHER AND PLATOFF, THE
TINY BONE CARVINGS BY FRENCH PRISONERS-
OF-WAR FROM PERTH AND EDINBURGH.

The Duke's brother, Lord George Murray, invented a
system of semaphore which was adopted by the
Admiralty. He also raised a volunteer force to defend the
south coast. Enthused perhaps by events in Europe, the
4th Duke, also known as the Planting Duke, is said to
have used a cannon to disperse the seed for the 25
million larch trees he planted.

On a more peaceable note, the delightful conversation
piece of the 4th Duke with his wife Jane Cathcart and
children was painted by David Allan. It clearly shows the
Georgian mansion in the background. The portrait over
the door is of the 4th Duke's nephew, George Murray,
Bishop of Rochester, who is the great-great-grandfather
of the 11th Duke.

The Book Room

THIS WAS ORIGINALLY THE DRESSING ROOM
TO THE RED BEDROOM. NOW IT HOUSES A
SMALL SELECTION OF BOOKS CONNECTED
WITH THE CASTLE.

Lord George Murray, the 1st Duke's youngest son (not to
be confused with the 4th Duke's brother of the same
name, above), owned the large part of them and took
them into exile with him in Holland after the '45. The
large oak fronted book case is made of wood from Castle
Rushen in the Isle of Man. The Atholl family connection
with the Isle of Man is explained more fully in the context
of the next two rooms, the Derby Suite.

The 4th Duke of Atholl and Family by David Allan

The 4th Duke is seen proudly displaying a blackcock to his delighted daughter after returning from a hunting excursion with his keeper, Alexander Crerar, and dogs. His first wife, Jane Cathcart, and their other children look on. In the background is the castle as it appeared from 1758, when the 2nd Duke completed the work of remodelling it as a grand Georgian mansion. It remained unaltered in this state for slightly over 100 years.

The Derby Suite

THESE TWO ROOMS ARE NAMED AFTER LADY AMELIA STANLEY, DAUGHTER OF THE 7TH EARL OF DERBY. LADY AMELIA MARRIED THE 1ST MARQUIS OF ATHOLL IN 1659.

Like all the best dynastic marriages this increased the family's wealth and influence, and it is through Amelia that her grandson, the 2nd Duke, later inherited the sovereignty of the Isle of Man. More recently, Queen Victoria used the Derby Suite during her visit in 1844, although with specially purchased furniture which is now in the Banvie Room.

THE DRESSING ROOM

This room has the rather odd distinction of being furnished almost entirely in broomwood, or rather a veneer made of pressed broom stalks.

The 3rd Duke was a keen proponent of this experimental approach to furniture design, but the fashion did not catch on. The cabinet (above) was made for him by Sandeman's of Perth in 1758. The matching scale model of a Roman temple is in fact a coin cabinet.

SANDEMAN'S ORIGINAL BILL FOR THE CABINET. IT COST THE 3RD DUKE TWENTY-ONE GUINEAS

DETAILS OF THE 17TH CENTURY
BED HANGING EMBROIDERIES:

THE DERBY ROOM

In 1650, during the Civil War, Lady Amelia Stanley's mother - Charlotte de la Tremouille, 7th Countess of Derby - found herself besieged in the family home, Latham House in Lancashire. As great ladies did in those days, she soothed her nerves by embroidering the bed hangings. Most of the rest of the furniture in the room is much later, however. The bed itself was made by Hepplewhite in the late 18th century. The Carlton House writing table was made by Gillow of Lancaster and the scrolled cabinet by Chipchase.

18TH CENTURY MOTHER-OF-PEARL BOWL AND EWER

A MID-18TH CENTURY PIEDMONTESE ROSEWOOD AND WALNUT CABINET, INLAID WITH IVORY AND MOTHER-OF-PEARL

FAR RIGHT: GEORGE III MAHOGANY CABINET VENEERED WITH ROSEWOOD

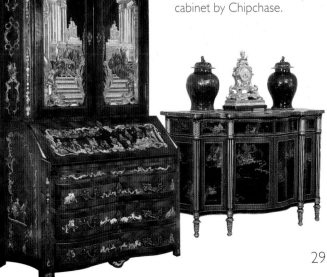

GILDED BUST OF THE 2ND DUKE
BY JOHN CHEERE

ON THE TABLE IN THE FOREGROUND ARE
PARIS BISQUE PORCELAIN FIGURES

The Red Bedroom

THE SPLENDID SCARLET BED, CHAIRS AND
STOOL IN THIS ROOM ARE PART OF A LARGER
SET BOUGHT FROM WILLIAM MASTERS BY THE
2ND DUKE IN 1756.

The room was last slept in by Crown Prince Hirohito of
Japan, when he visited Blair Castle in 1921, one of the
very last in the long line of distinguished guests who have
stayed at the castle over the centuries.

DETAIL FROM THE PIER GLASS
CARVING; A SQUIRREL
MUNCHING ON AN ACORN

The gilded bust of the 2nd Duke is
by John Cheere who also made the
statue of Hercules in the grounds.
The portraits by Jeremiah Davison
and Allan Ramsay are of the Duke's
Whig friends.

TARTAN PLAID UNIFORM OF THE
ROYAL COMPANY OF ARCHERS

The Drawing Room

AFTER THE BALLROOM
THIS IS THE LARGEST
ROOM IN THE CASTLE.
IT CERTAINLY
REPRESENTS THE
PINNACLE OF THE 2ND
DUKE'S ASPIRATIONS TO
GRANDEUR.

Picture it candlelit with the
crimson damask shimmering
on the walls, firelight reflected
in the pier glass mirrors and
glinting off the gilt work. It
would have been a magnificent
room in which to entertain.

DETAIL FROM THE PAINTING
BY JOHANN ZOFFANY OF
THE 3RD DUKE AND HIS
FAMILY

Thomas Clayton produced his most elaborate work here,
on the ceiling and cornice, and Thomas Carter another
marble chimneypiece which sets off the outstanding
picture of the 3rd Duke and his family by Johann
Zoffany. The boy standing next to his father in the

CHINESE POTTERY HAWK
AND SILVER QUAICH

conversation piece is John, later the 4th Duke, whose portrait as an adult, by John Hoppner, hangs beside the fireplace. A portrait of his second wife, Marjory Forbes, also by Hoppner, hangs on the other side. The boy on the extreme right in the Zoffany picture, Lord George, was the common ancestor of the 10th and 11th Dukes.

The Drawing Room furniture is a connoisseur's delight. It includes the Louis XVI gilt chairs and settees by Chipchase, and the larchwood regency cabinets on either side of the fireplace, made for the 4th Duke by Bullock of Liverpool. The damask wall covering was replaced in the 19th century and again in the 1970s. Small sections of the original remain around the Cole pier glass mirrors, (illustrated overleaf).

THE 4TH DUKE BY JOHN HOPPNER

THE CHIPCHASE LOUIS XVI FURNITURE HAS NEEDLEWORK UPHOLSTERY WORKED BY LADY CHARLOTTE, DAUGHTER OF THE 3RD DUKE, SEEN HERE HOLDING THE WREATH

THE TARTAN ON THE TENT BED IS SUPPOSED TO HAVE COME FROM AN OLDER CIRCULAR BED IN WHICH, FEET OUT, SLEPT THE 17 SONS OF SIR DAVID MURRAY OF TULLIBARDINE

PRINCE CHARLES EDWARD STUART
'BONNIE PRINCE CHARLIE'

CUMMING'S TOWER

The Tullibardine Room

LEGEND HAS IT THAT PRINCE CHARLES EDWARD STUART USED THIS ROOM WHEN HE STAYED AT BLAIR CASTLE IN 1745.

A 15th century addition to Cumming's Tower, the room is dedicated to the Jacobite members of the Atholl family and is named after William, Marquis of Tullibardine, the 1st Duke's son, whose support for the Stewarts led to the forfeiture of his claim to the dukedom and estates.

A portrait of his younger brother, Lord George Murray who was the Prince's celebrated Lieutenant General, hangs by the entrance door. Lord George was pardoned after his involvement in the 1715 rising, although he stubbornly joined the cause again in the '45 and died eventually in exile in Holland. His pardon for his part in the '15 can be seen by the window.

AN 18TH CENTURY PORTRAIT OF LORD GEORGE MURRAY, WITH THE PARDON FOR HIS PART IN THE 1715 RISING

They were spotted in Paris and bought for the 1st Duke, then still Marquis of Tullibardine, who had them brought home to hang in this second floor room of Cumming's Tower.

The spectacular William and Mary state bed, with its Spitalfields silk hangings and ostrich plumes, says much for the 1st Duke's sense of his own status. It was brought to Blair Castle from Holyrood where, prior to his arrest for opposing the Act of Union, the 1st Duke kept an apartment as Lord Privy Seal to the Scottish Parliament.

19TH CENTURY MANTEL CLOCK THOUGHT TO HAVE BELONGED TO CARDINAL RICHELIEU

The Tapestry Room

ROYAL MISFORTUNE WAS THE ATHOLL FAMILY'S GOOD FORTUNE WHEN CROMWELL ORDERED CHARLES I'S FINE MORTLAKE TAPESTRIES TO BE SOLD FOLLOWING HIS EXECUTION.

MORTLAKE TAPESTRY ILLUSTRATING A WILD BOAR HUNT

THE 1ST DUKE'S DESPATCH BOX, USED IN THE SCOTTISH PARLIAMENT PRIOR TO 1707, WAS LOST ON HIS DEATH AND SUBSEQUENTLY FOUND BY THE 7TH DUKE IN AN EDINBURGH CURIOSITY SHOP

The adjoining dressing room has portraits of the 1st Duke's two wives, Lady Katherine Hamilton and Mary Ross, along with one each of their daughters

The Banvie Suite

IT MUST HAVE BEEN A WELCOME MOMENT
WHEN GUESTS COULD RETREAT FROM THE
FORMAL GRANDEUR OF THE DOWNSTAIRS
ROOMS TO THE COMFORT OF THIS
ATTRACTIVE VICTORIAN BEDROOM SUITE.

Most of the carved oak furniture was bought for the visit
of Queen Victoria in 1844, although she actually used
downstairs rooms during her stay. The pictures show the
2nd Lord Glenlyon, later the 6th Duke, reviewing
the Atholl Highlanders at Dunkeld. Also his wife,
Anne Home Drummond, who was the Queen's
friend, Lady-in-waiting and Mistress of the Robes.

The next generation is fully represented in the dressing room. This has a small painting of the 7th Duke on china, portraits of his wife, Louisa Moncrieffe, and her seven sisters, and watercolours of their six children.

The terracotta statuette of Queen Victoria at her spinning wheel, presented by the Queen to the 6th Duchess in 1869, is the model for a silver statuette that can be seen in the ballroom at Balmoral.

SIR EDWIN LANDSEER PAINTED THIS CHARMING PORTRAIT OF THE YOUNG JAMES MURRAY, BROTHER OF THE 2ND LORD GLENLYON, WITH JOHN McMILLAN, A FISHERMAN. IT HANGS IN THE GLENLYON LOBBY THROUGH WHICH ONE ENTERS THE BANVIE SUITE

THE 2ND LORD GLENLYON, LATER THE 6TH DUKE, REVIEWING THE ATHOLL HIGHLANDERS AT DUNKELD

The models of figures at a highland games can also be seen in silver at Balmoral. They represent a number of the original highland challenges which still take place at the Atholl Gathering, the highland games held each summer in the castle grounds.

In the Banvie turret, memorabilia belonging to Lord Tullibardine, later the 8th Duke, and his wife, bring the family into the 20th century.

TERRACOTTA STATUETTE OF QUEEN VICTORIA AT A SPINNING WHEEL, WITH A BUST OF PRINCE ALBERT

The Treasure Room

PEOPLE'S PERSONAL POSSESSIONS REVEAL MUCH ABOUT THE WAY THEY LIVED. THE TREASURE ROOM OFFERS A RARE GLIMPSE OF ATHOLL FAMILY HISTORY THROUGH THE MICROSCOPE.

Some of the items on display have been lovingly collected, others are simply everyday objects that have gained interest through the passage of time.

Amongst the enormous array of jewellery, personal mementoes, games, seals and other memorabilia of bygone ages, there are a collection of Jacobite relics brought together by the 7th Duke, and a number of miniatures collected by the 9th Duke who also painted some of them himself.

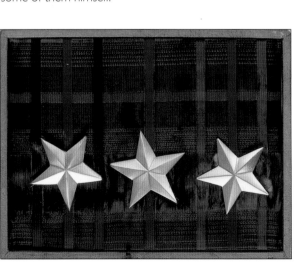

LEFT: SILVER-MOUNTED QUAICH, WITH A PENANNULAR HIGHLAND BROOCH

PORTOBELLO WARE FIGURINES c. 1760

LADY CHARLOTTE ANNE MURRAY'S SILVER RATTLE

CANTON ENAMEL SHELL-SHAPED SNUFF BOX c. 1740

19TH CENTURY CAMEO TIARA, WITH A CLASSICAL GREEK TABLEAU

SEAL RING WITH THE IMPRESSION OF CHARLES EDWARD STUART 'BONNIE PRINCE CHARLIE'

IVORY COMPASS ONCE USED BY CHARLES EDWARD STUART

LEFT: THE MURRAY STARS

RAM'S HORN SNUFFBOX DECORATED WITH SILVER AND JEWELS

17TH CENTURY GUNPOWDER HORN

The next generation is fully represented in the dressing room. This has a small painting of the 7th Duke on china, portraits of his wife, Louisa Moncrieffe, and her seven sisters, and watercolours of their six children.

The terracotta statuette of Queen Victoria at her spinning wheel, presented by the Queen to the 6th Duchess in 1869, is the model for a silver statuette that can be seen in the ballroom at Balmoral.

TERRACOTTA STATUETTE OF QUEEN VICTORIA AT A SPINNING WHEEL, WITH A BUST OF PRINCE ALBERT

SIR EDWIN LANDSEER PAINTED THIS CHARMING PORTRAIT OF THE YOUNG JAMES MURRAY, BROTHER OF THE 2ND LORD GLENLYON, WITH JOHN McMILLAN, A FISHERMAN. IT HANGS IN THE GLENLYON LOBBY THROUGH WHICH ONE ENTERS THE BANVIE SUITE

THE 2ND LORD GLENLYON, LATER THE 6TH DUKE, REVIEWING THE ATHOLL HIGHLANDERS AT DUNKELD

The models of figures at a highland games can also be seen in silver at Balmoral. They represent a number of the original highland challenges which still take place at the Atholl Gathering, the highland games held each summer in the castle grounds.

In the Banvie turret, memorabilia belonging to Lord Tullibardine, later the 8th Duke, and his wife, bring the family into the 20th century.

The Front Staircase

THE FINE CARVED STAIRCASE, WHICH WAS DESIGNED FOR THE 2ND DUKE BY ABRAHAM SWAN, IS HOME TO VARIOUS CURIOSITIES SUCH AS THE NARWHAL TUSK AND THE PREHISTORIC SKULL OF AN IRISH ELK THAT MIGHT SEEM INCONGRUOUS, IF NOT ALARMING, IN OTHER PARTS OF THE CASTLE.

It also has two attractive portraits. The first is of young James Moray of Abercairney, probably painted in the period after the '45 when the kilt was proscribed, which would explain why the picture is not signed. The second is of the 4th Duke's youngest son, Lord Charles Murray, who died, like Byron, in the cause of Greek independence. Like his parents in the Drawing Room, Lord Charles was painted by Hoppner.

ABOVE: JAMES MORAY OF ABERCAIRNEY

LORD CHARLES MURRAY, THE 4TH DUKE'S YOUNGEST SON BY HOPPNER

JOUSTING ARMOUR MADE IN 1839 FOR LORD GLENLYON, LATER 6TH DUKE, TO WEAR AT THE EGLINTON TOURNAMENT, A RECREATION OF A MEDIEVAL JOUST IN AYRSHIRE. THE PRESENT ATHOLL HIGHLANDERS ORIGINATE FROM THE BODYGUARD HE TOOK WITH HIM TO THE TOURNAMENT.

The Atholl Highlanders Room

The Atholl Highlanders today enjoy the extraordinary distinction of being the only private army in Europe. But this does not mean that they are available to fight at the personal behest of their colonel, the Duke of Atholl ! In reality they would only ever do so in the service of Queen and Country.

The Atholl Highlanders were first raised in 1778 by the 4th Duke as a regular military regiment. It was intended that they should fight in the American War of Independence, but after some disagreement they were eventually posted to Ireland instead, and later disbanded.

After many years in abeyance, the regiment was revived in 1966 by the 10th Duke and now parades at the castle each year in the presence of its colonel, the 11th Duke. The displays in the Atholl Highlanders Room trace the regiment's history from 1778 to the present day.

The current regiment dates from 1839 when Lord Glenlyon took a bodyguard of men to the medieval tournament at Eglinton in Ayrshire. Five years later, he arranged for the Atholl Highlanders to mount guard when Queen Victoria stayed at Blair Castle. For this service they were granted her colours and so the right to bear arms.

ATHOLL HIGHLANDERS PARADE IN FRONT OF THE CASTLE, WITH THE 6TH DUKE'S SILVER MOUNTED SPORRAN, AND A SET OF EARLY 18TH CENTURY BAGPIPES

JOHN, 11TH DUKE OF ATHOLL INSPECTING HIS PRIVATE ARMY OF ATHOLL HIGHLANDERS; HIS POSITION AS CHIEFTAIN IS INDICATED BY THE GOLDEN EAGLE FEATHER IN HIS GLENGARRY CAP

LEFT: SILVER-MOUNTED QUAICH, WITH A PENANNULAR HIGHLAND BROOCH

PORTOBELLO WARE FIGURINES c. 1760

The Treasure Room

PEOPLE'S PERSONAL POSSESSIONS REVEAL MUCH ABOUT THE WAY THEY LIVED. THE TREASURE ROOM OFFERS A RARE GLIMPSE OF ATHOLL FAMILY HISTORY THROUGH THE MICROSCOPE.

Some of the items on display have been lovingly collected, others are simply everyday objects that have gained interest through the passage of time.

Amongst the enormous array of jewellery, personal mementoes, games, seals and other memorabilia of bygone ages, there are a collection of Jacobite relics brought together by the 7th Duke, and a number of miniatures collected by the 9th Duke who also painted some of them himself.

LADY CHARLOTTE ANNE MURRAY'S SILVER RATTLE

CANTON ENAMEL SHELL-SHAPED SNUFF BOX c. 1740

19TH CENTURY CAMEO TIARA, WITH A CLASSICAL GREEK TABLEAU

SEAL RING WITH THE IMPRESSION OF CHARLES EDWARD STUART 'BONNIE PRINCE CHARLIE'

IVORY COMPASS ONCE USED BY CHARLES EDWARD STUART

LEFT: THE MURRAY STARS

RAM'S HORN SNUFFBOX DECORATED WITH SILVER AND JEWELS

17TH CENTURY GUNPOWDER HORN

The dolls, games, toys, clothes, furniture and furnishings have all played their part in the childhood of various members of the Atholl family. They include the 10th Duke's christening robe which hangs in the cupboard.

TOY YACHT GIFTED TO THE 10TH DUKE

The Nursery

THIS SCENE FROM A VICTORIAN CHILD'S NURSERY HAS BEEN RECREATED ENTIRELY FROM ITEMS DISCOVERED AT DIFFERENT TIMES THROUGHOUT THE CASTLE.

Aviemore Photographic

The Ballroom

MORE THAN A HUNDRED YEARS AFTER IT
WAS BUILT, THIS MAGNIFICENT ROOM STILL
ECHOES TO THE SOUND OF PIPES, FIDDLES
AND DANCING AT THE HIGHLAND BALLS,
WEDDING RECEPTIONS AND GRAND PARTIES
FOR WHICH IT IS FREQUENTLY USED TODAY.

Aviemore Photographic

THE ANNUAL
KEEPERS OF THE
QUAICH DINNER,
TRADITIONALLY
HELD IN THE
BALLROOM

Aviemore Photographic

The 7th Duke added the ballroom in 1876 for the annual
gathering of the Atholl Highlanders at which they
commemorated the granting of their colours. His portrait
hangs above the stage. The stags' heads that keep him
company around the room have all been shot on the
extensive Atholl estate which has a long and scrupulous
tradition of red deer management.

To right and left of the door are portraits of the 8th Duke, as Marquis of Tullibardine, and his wife Katharine Ramsay, Scotland's first woman MP. To the right of the musicians' gallery is the famous sporting picture by Sir Edwin Landseer, *Death of a Hart in Glen Tilt.*

Niel Gow
and
his fiddle

Appropriately positioned above the stage is Sir Henry Raeburn's portrait of Niel Gow, the celebrated fiddler and composer to the 2nd, 3rd and 4th Dukes. Gow's music is still much played today. His fiddle is displayed in the case and brought out on special occasions.

The China Room

CHOOSING THE RIGHT TABLEWARE AND NOT
BREAKING IT MUST HAVE BEEN SOMETHING OF
A HEADACHE FOR CASTLE STAFF IN EARLIER
DAYS. THERE ARE OVER 1700 PIECES OF
CHINA IN THIS ROOM,
SPECIALLY CONVERTED
FROM A FORMER
KITCHEN COURTYARD BY
THE 7TH DUKE.

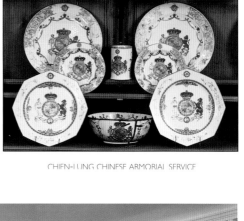

CHIEN-LUNG CHINESE ARMORIAL SERVICE

CHIEN-LUNG CHINESE ARMORIAL PLATE
SHOWING THE ATHOLL ARMS

The stunning collection includes
a Coalport set painted by
Amelia, daughter of the 4th
Duke, and the blue Dresden set
given to the 6th Duchess as a
wedding present by her father
in 1839.

COALPORT CHINA
PAINTED BY AMELIA,
DAUGHTER OF THE
4TH DUKE

ETRUSCAN PLATTER

The Embroidery Display

THE NEEDLEWORK IN THIS REMARKABLE
DISPLAY WAS EITHER WORKED OR
COLLECTED BY THE SCHOLARLY AND
RECLUSIVE LADY EVELYN MURRAY, YOUNGEST
DAUGHTER OF THE 7TH DUKE.

After a teenage illness, Lady Evelyn began to study
Gaelic and collect folk stories from all over highland
Perthshire. But having moved to Switzerland for her
health, she decided eventually not to return to
Scotland, and settled instead in Belgium where she took
up needlework. The exquisite armorial panel which
forms the centrepiece is Lady Evelyn's own work, and is
considered to be one of the finest examples of 20th
century British embroidery. She sent her collection
back to Scotland in 1936, shortly before returning
herself to Perthshire where she died in 1940.

LADY EVELYN'S MASTERPIECE 'THE BRITISH ARMS'

Haste ye back!

FAMILY HISTORY IS NOT ALL THAT BLAIR CASTLE HAS TO OFFER. WE HOPE THAT YOUR TOUR OF THE ROOMS WILL HAVE WHETTED YOUR APPETITE FOR EVERYTHING ELSE THERE IS TO DO AND SEE HERE.

Your first stop will probably be the shop or restaurant. The shop has a wide range of books and souvenirs, many based on the Blair Castle collection. The restaurant serves a choice of meals and refreshments. Both are open all day.

Outside, you will see that successive Dukes of Atholl lavished as much care on their natural surroundings as they did on the castle itself. Take your time to explore and enjoy the castle grounds, with their formal landscapes, fine statuary and magnificent trees.

Further afield, but still within the boundaries of the Atholl estates, there are waymarked trails, pony trekking and a variety of other sporting opportunities.

The estate ranger service can advise on walks and other activities, and there are guide books on sale in the shop. The rangers' information centre is in the village, opposite the caravan park.

Blair Castle also hosts two popular annual events. The last weekend in May sees the Atholl Gathering, with the annual parade of the Atholl Highlanders, followed by the traditional Highland Games. Then in August there are the International Horse Trials, a major equestrian event.